Black Nostalgia

"Stories Untold"

S. Lynn Garner

Black Nostalgia   S. Lynn Garner

Black Nostalgia   S. Lynn Garner

ISBN: 9798657521429

Cover design by: S. Lynn Garner
Library of Congress Control Number: 2018675309
Printed in the United States of America

I dedicate my most heartfelt, and authentic expressions, to my eternal first loves: My beautiful mother, Louise Marie, and amazing father, Kenneth Joseph.

With love and honor,

Your daughter, forever.

"We delight in the beauty of the butterfly,
but rarely admit the changes it has gone
through to achieve that beauty."

-Maya Angelou

Contents

Black Nostalgia   S. Lynn Garner

Black Nostalgia   S. Lynn Garner

Preface

Before you begin, this intimate journey with

me, I invite you to open your hearts to a

time, once forgotten. With the multitude of

tasks that impact our lives daily, we rarely

get to explore our deepest, most vulnerable

thoughts, unaccompanied by the fear of

judgement. Moreover, we are swamped with

insignificant insecurities of inadequacy,

which inevitably leads to our complacent

behavior, and our untimely, internal demise.

Through poetry, I release striking, yet

transparent content, while embracing the

spirit of discernment, truth and most

importantly, gratitude. It is my hope that you

embrace, and honor your passions, in order

to grow mentally, and spiritually. Mental

and spiritual growth is the foundation for

true progress.

"The foundation we build at this very

moment, will undoubtedly hold the key to

our future success or failure. In order to

truly value the art of progress, failure must

be welcomed and expected."

-S. Lynn Garner

*"You can never enslave
somebody who knows who
he is."*

-Alex Haley

Black Nostalgia   S. Lynn Garner

Black Nostalgia   S. Lynn Garner

Black Nostalgia

Gritty, uneven, historic - stricken streets,

Leave rowdy kids with bruised,

Bumped and tender knees.

The screaming bright, yet deceitful skies,

Tell stories of our ancestors –

From the start of time.

A simple, windy, delicate breeze,

Brings back stark imagery;

Like early 90s wind breakers suits…

A time once keen.

Spring soon recedes,

While mischievous, free-spirited lads

Black Nostalgia   S. Lynn Garner

Scream,

A fiery flame soon erupts…

As hot, sticky sweat,

Drip slowly down-

Cocoa butter, smooth,

Supple cheeks

And Vaseline graced,

Cherry cool-cup lips;

…filled with neighborhood coated sweets

Blue birds begin to chirp,

While we're laced in the latest

Ripped white, spray painted t-shirts,

Paired with exclusive raw denim shorts

Or maybe summer-time skirts.

As Texas mosquitos bite the day

Away,

And leave fluid filled, red, itchy,

Annoying bumps,

Onn our legs and arms

To marinate-

While, staining memories of a time,

So free,

So at ease,

So at peace.

The street light yells for us to come in,

And soothe our war wounds of the day,

Oops…

We've tarnished our ice white

Tennis shoes…

Our mothers are pissed, and possibly,

Throwing a fit;

But we still reminisce...

Black Nostalgia   S. Lynn Garner

And silently smile in delight,

While recalling the day...

Our hearts are stuffed with warm

Memories of hide and seek, tag,

Scraped knees, and

God's radiant sun rays...

But, this moment in time soon ends,

While the falling season begins...

Simple, yet invigorating sounds

Of laughter and play,

Slowly evaporate

Into broken smiles,

And complete disarray.

We gradually dissipate

And grow away,

Yet-

To our dismay,

In those simple, small,

Still moments…

We eventually stay.

Black Nostalgia   S. Lynn Garner

Black Nostalgia   S. Lynn Garner

Black Nostalgia   S. Lynn Garner

Muse

Ethereally thrilling,

Benevolent, yet deceiving,

Euphorically pleasing,

Endlessly competing,

Effortlessly achieving,

Stimulating

Forever contemplating,

Feel free to liberate thee…...

or even,

Enlighten thy senses,

Massage my thoughts without fear,

Twisted dreams of elation and dread,

You're truly cutting edge,

Heated hearts beat profusely,

Distinctive clarity,

Your truth embodies a burning mind of

Steel;

Yet,

Trapped with...

Intellectual desires,

You ne'er tire....

Keep inspiring.

For,

You're my muse.

Shall I ever refuse?

With you by my side...

I shall never lose.

Ambition

Broken Silhouette

As I gaze at the broken, muted

Yet, perfect frame,

I can't help, but notice,

The unequal distribution,

Which immediately…

Overwhelms the wholesome, yet weakly-

Shape

The shape that holds fiery desire,

Fear,

Lies,

Indecent thoughts...

Fill the void with ease,

Supple, pretty days go by,

And heavy, black nights,

Sweep the rustic streets,

With one smooth breeze,

Not feeling a thing,

Yet, longing to be free,

Keeping maximum distance,

But still fighting to see,

Broken promises,

Broken dreams,

Broken hope,

Still comes with a fee,

Know who you are,

And love who you see.

Black Nostalgia   S. Lynn Garner

Passive

Coping with quarreling thoughts,

Mixed emotionless, breathless hearts,

Broken inspiration,

Silent lips,

Closed ears,

Inhumane feelings….

As we hear...

Crippled opinions, brought on by fears.

Hostage, hopeless nights,

Instantly become clear...

Should I fight?

Should I reflect?

Should I break?

Or

Remain closed lip?

Neglect my thoughts, hopes,

Perspectives?

To sustain your weapon?

Weapon of manipulation!

Which only leads to mass insecurity,

And destruction!

Never fleeing,

Only breeding,

Solid energy,

Speak out…courageously,

Plant your seed.

Black Nostalgia   S. Lynn Garner

Black Thoughts

Be all you can be!

Is this a joke?

Doesn't that sound like some dumb shit?

Being the best doesn't apply to me!

This can't be real…

You see…

They're not genuinely interested in me.

I'm the best ever and still will never be

Seen…

Get this degree,

That one, and that one too!

But-

You still will need to play the fool.

Neglect your inner self

Be an imitation of them,

Change your tone!

Hair texture too!

Caged in…

(Zoo)

Be a distant memory,

Trust me…it's coming soon,

And don't think alone,

Just do what you're told,

Never be bold!

And you just might win.

Keyword - MIGHT!

But, what really is the win?

…

The letdown of my people,

The letdown of my freedom,

Or the greatest letdown of all,

Self...

All for eternal sin.

You see,

Naturally born me,

And all I can be,

Only applies,

When I finally realize,

My definition of self-worthy success,

Belongs to me.

Rotten Red

Healthy,

But

Vicious….

What a decision?

Strong, yet fragile,

Naturally gorgeous…

Yet,

Undoubtedly rotten

Once you penetrate

The inner core,

Simply – complex

The first pick of the day,

Monumental cliché,

Consistently trending,

Polished,

And unequal

Still a beautiful bore,

But could never ignore…

The immaculate view,

Until you choke

On manipulative anecdotes,

Provoked--

By the rotten,

Deceitful,

Inner core.

Black Nostalgia   S. Lynn Garner

Queen

Luscious, yet

Destructive,

Mahogany rich,

Smooth mocha chocolate,

Melts hearts from past decades

On end.

Pure caramel -- swirled into

A decadent delight,

Sweet,

Vanilla bean,

Cinnamon based dream.

A pinch of nutmeg,

A cup of brown sugar,

A teaspoon of dark, pure vanilla,

Mixed into…

A golden, sun-kissed,

Supple, bronzed, cocoa butter,

Glistening,

Masterpiece.

Who -- moves!

Which entices anyone to sin.

Perfectly slender,

Roasted almond,

Butter pecan,

Coco - hazelnut,

eyes,

Is where her truth, truly lies….

Graciously curved,

Sweet honey coated,

Ripe, hypnotizing lips…

Will tell stories,

From the first original creation

And ignite flames to mend.

Deep, distinctive,

Soul

Buries historic royal bloodlines

Unsold.

The naturally deep, flirtatious back arch

Creates a strategic small...

Which sits at

The edge of her back,

Draws you further towards sin

Whilst,

Waist,

Will tranquilize demons,

Tantalizing thoughts to sin.

Bronzed glow,

Sings a royal soul;

A mahogany goddess you are!

With legs of pyramids

Following the midnight star.

Endearing, yet intimate,

S - shaped

Purely arched

Golden, famed feet,

Will bind the devil

When she walks

Which forces him to flee!

You see…

Her naturally - beautiful - physicality

Will always be,

A temporary source of empty,

Unsubstantial fulfillment,

Only for the shallow world to

Envy,

But it's her timeless

CROWN,

Her depth of internal wealth,

Her strength…

Her unparalleled dignity,

Never compromising self,

For anyone or anything

Else,

If she allows herself

To break shackles

And chains of deceit…

And never succumb to defeat;

The original

Queen

Is

Instantly

Freed.

Black Nostalgia   S. Lynn Garner

Creole

As a child I never really understood,

A culture so rich,

So influential,

Yet, still misunderstood.

You see,

Growing up,

With a dose of extra

Magnificent Melanin,

In my skin…

I never seemed to match,

Because a fair-skinned mom and sister,

Graced our family patch,

I didn't relate,

Nor did I try,

Yet, spent countless nights,

Asking the Lord why?

Why this?

Why that?

Am I adopted or just a beautiful defect?

But the truth was evident….

Our people are built strong

Through trials and tribulations

Rape and manipulation

Our shades are so strong

Which brings distinctive pride

So we carry on.

Shades never mattered in my home,

I was loved so richly and completely,

Considered an instant treasure,

And a recurrent lesson

Of our ancestors

And a sweet piece of history…

I just thought we should have,

The picture perfect family image,

Where we all looked exactly the same…

You know...

Like most white families...

On the TV screen…

A youthful,

Idle mind,

Will overthink and subconsciously hide,

Internal feelings and thoughts,

Of one sided pride,

Obviously with a dark side,

Make no mistake.

My heart,

Is where…

My creole blood runs rapidly,

And will always reside

No matter the shade

Which beautifully graces,

The

Outside.

Black Nostalgia   S. Lynn Garner

S. Lynn Garner

Empty Pleasures

Deep rooted selfish pleasures,

Fills the dark,

Endless void,

Sin devours broken thoughts,

To no end,

To hope or not,

Is to breathe or die,

Shallow images cling,

To hopeless dreams on end,

To love... and to lose,

Is to live without breath,

Sunny days ahead,

But leads to a fiery,

Death.

While nights bring the calm,

To live

And to not

Have desired,

Is to have sight,

Without an ounce of

Vison.

Black Nostalgia   S. Lynn Garner

Murky Waters

Murky waters glow,

As the moon brings light,

To the dark, lonely

Sky.

Forgotten memories drift,

As the sun shifts,

Hearts are left sunken,

Through waves and shadows,

Which drift…

of lost days….

With moments left behind,

Whilst,

Future plans are sought;

Sought to bring depth and new meaning,

To life,

Where does one begin?

The present is clear,

Past moments – still feared,

And the future...

Is still murky,

But,

The glow is ever clear.

Black Nostalgia  S. Lynn Garner

Black Nostalgia   S. Lynn Garner

Southern Magnolia

Strong and firm,

Glowingly,

Painstakingly gorgeous!

Not easily manipulated,

Simply gentle and at peace,

To see her beauty,

Is to see her sin,

Relentless, yet warm as gin,

Beauty is peacefully innate

And can never be defaced,

Thrives in all seasons

Timeless treason

Her mark is clear,

It is safe,

There will never be another,

To fill her place.

S. Lynn Garner

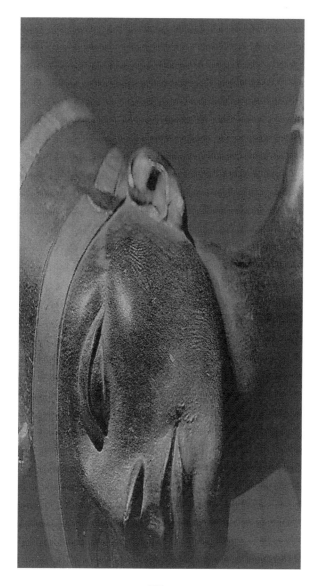

Abrasive

Not too loud!

Not too proud!

Watch your tone!

You can't make a sound,

You can't be too confident,

Nor too smart,

Passion is overrated;

Don't speak from your heart,

But you can speak…

When you are spoken to--

AND only with permission

You see….

Your face gives the wrong impression,

You are seen as too bold!

Your look is intimidating,

It gives off the impression of an

Immediate threat,

Work on taking it down a notch,

Make sure you blend in,

But ohhhh,

Let Ben take charge,

You see...

It's expected for him to be aggressive,

Doesn't matter if you both possess the

Same viewpoints

Or college degrees,

Just agree and move on,

No need to seek answers,

79

And cause strife…

Which spark fights

And maybe riots…

And unnecessary HR filing,

And you officially become the

Outlier.

Oh and Karen…

Just let her be passionate and brave,

She's just speaking from her heart,

She always going to legally use her

Voice.

But you….

You see,

Your skin is black.

Soul runs deep.

Historically marked

Features strategically distinct.

Abrasive from the start.

Black Nostalgia   S. Lynn Garner

S. Lynn Garner

Brownstone

Timeless and intricate,

Profoundly understated,

Rich exterior layers,

And a deep harvested culture,

Influenced by history

And created by design,

Crafted through luxury,

And polished with pride,

Yet, the untold story is…

Rugged,

Built with hearty grit,

And soulful pride,

Rough hands endure

Tough souls pursue,

Yet…

Long for,

A place to call home.

S. Lynn Garner

Time

You are innocent, yet cruel,

Tempting and rude,

Present is your focus,

The past is instantly unnoticed,

You break bonds,

And tarnish memories,

You're thoughtless,

Yet-

Persistently considerate…

Provoking!

Never looking back,

Tenaciously, on track

Relentless you are,

Local and afar,

Focused,

Organized and stark,

But, most importantly…

short.

Black Nostalgia   S. Lynn Garner

Bridging The Gap

Warm thoughts.

Silent cries.

Blurry pride.

As you soon realize,

Grace is priceless.

While spirit is,

Earned.

Peace is precious.

Yet-

Still taken for granted.

The gap is wide.

You must decide.

To bridge

or to…

let go.

Black Nostalgia   S. Lynn Garner

Selective Thoughts

Drown infiltrated thoughts

And stolen plans of the past,

With aspirations of the future,

Pick and choose wisely,

But, cut ties smoothly.

Unchain honest passions,

From internal prison cells,

Growth is desirable,

But never inevitable…...

Choose your path,

As the road,

Not taken,

Harness your goals,

Embrace your worth,

And the rest is merely,

to be,

Let go.

Black Nostalgia   S. Lynn Garner

Dark Alley

Gloomy,

Smoked filled

Disrupted skies,

The smell of ash,

Surrounds the pure night,

Cold, grimy, uneven pavements

Somehow balance my feet,

As I slip,

And reminisce…

To a more delightful time,

Of warm,

Fresh cut,

Bright, green grass…

Overwhelming my senses,

As I swallow the day,

The clouds hide the illuminating light,

From the sun - briefly,

While pedestrians stroll eagerly;

On their way,

The day eventually sets;

Leaving a golden,

Temporary mark

To stay.

And yet again,

I'll be on my way.

S. Lynn Garner

Assumption

Second guessing,

Constantly contemplating,

Always with a preconceived answer,

Never a break,

Completing sentences,

And phrases

Before the start.

Hoping to come to grips,

With my secret thoughts

Never idle-

Crucially vital…

Yearning for more,

Pleading to think,

But…eventually falling apart,

Learning to cope,

Progressing with hope,

Starting to block,

Unproductive thoughts.

Black Nostalgia   S. Lynn Garner

Misguided

Accepting some form of truth,

through....

Deceptive realities,

Neglectful,

Distorted blunders,

Controlling pathways,

While bringing us further apart,

Denying all logic;

Such a distant voice,

Driven to terms,

With the fact,

That…

You are the answer,

Since,

Taunting thoughts,

Haunts the soul,

But,

Becomes clueless

As the wrath unfolds,

Wake up before it's too late!

And learn from

empty

mistakes.

Ignite

Passions draws near,

Without the doubt of fear,

Dreams stand firm,

Lacking a dose of concern,

Flames ignite,

Despite the lack of sight,

Victory is clear,

As you cast away fears,

Breaking shackles to free…

Your soul from bleeding.

Learning to grow,

And progressing with courage,

Becomes your sole source

of strength,

You are your best shot,

So never neglect to:

Invest,

Inspire,

And most importantly…

Re-hire

Because your success

Is only as significant

As your brothers

Left behind

But want so desperately,

To be alive

And rise

And live the dream

You own-

You are not your own.

So,

Never disown

Always

Ignite.

Black Nostalgia

S. Lynn Garner

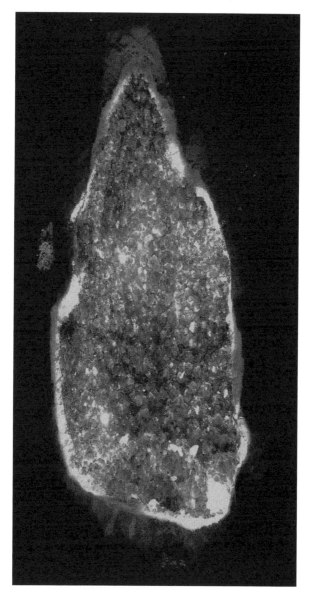

Black Diamonds

Sharp edges.

Tragic start.

Opaque heart.

They wonder why your thoughts are so

Dark.

Never forgetting your background.

Regardless of the ups, but mostly

Downs.

Working as twice as hard,

To shine as bright,

As your white,

Naturally, illuminating peers.

Digging deeper in fear.

Feeling the disparities, consume your

Core,

Feeling as if …

You can't take anymore,

Long nights and days on the shelf,

While the white supremacist only care

For self,

Realizing you are seen as second rate,

And you can never win the race.

You see…

You started centuries behind,

But, the rule is for you to still comply,

With unfair standards and practices,

No matter who's asking,

You're expected to lose,

Without one sudden move.

Because "they" are intimidated,

Simply trying to obliterate you,

But here is the caveat;

you must remember,

They could NEVER!

Because you are designed for greatness,

Remember, you are the first creation,

Your brain is extra sharp,

And you will naturally leave your mark,

While glowing immaculately,

Against all odds

And preconceived ideology,

Never backing down,

And always profound,

You see…

You will always be,

Original;

Unmeasurable;

Breathtaking

Beyond the time of Beauty;

Radiantly - Resilient;

Strikingly – Supreme

Blossomly - Brilliant;

Devine.

But most importantly,

You are rare;

A true,

delicacy.

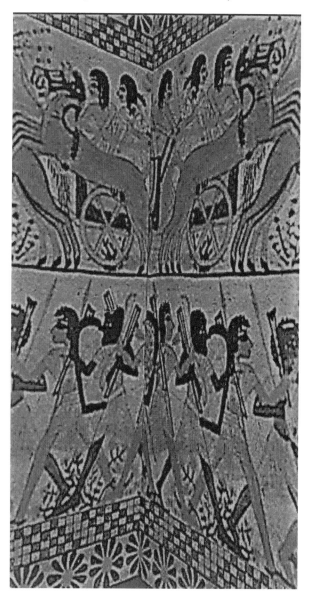

Pharaoh

Grounded in eternal hope…strength and

Dignity...

Graced with substance, and pure

Righteousness

And always adds value,

With a dose of hearty pride,

Clothed in wool, sheepskin, and fur

Laced in the best silk, and Pharaoh gold.

Models tenacity to no end

Internal instincts…as sharp as shattered

Sin,

Love is as tender,

As a soothing spirit;

Rarely known to man.

Provider of morals, distinctive values,

And guidance...

Protector of peace, innocence; honor

Foundation cemented, yet hammered

Into the sea,

Surpasses monumental struggles...

For his young to be.

While always believing, but never

Seeing...

The ultimate complexity--

Of the hard working black man story,

Hands made with stone,

Bones fused with courage;

Sweat of our ancestor pride

S. Lynn Garner

Drips slowly to his feet

Never broken,

Never borrowed,

Just stolen.

Stolen by deceit, pain; convoluted

Agony.

Lies compete…

Stories still untold- -

Memories near forgotten

While we observe history unfold...

Connection…a true virtue,

Never ending,

Still beginning,

His true name is King...

Never externally compromised

Nor… destroyed, with worldly bling

But,

His light is still bright...

So bright!

For the culture to see.

The skies fall....and rejoice!

With tears of joy

At the mere sight of your soul,

Demons depart,

As your royal feet marks

The ground so delicately...

Graced with a jubilant melody.

Heart of pure, solid,

Iridescent gold...

Confidence unfolds,

Naturally.

Simply because....

You are a Pharaoh.

Dad--

You could never be

sold.

Black Nostalgia   S. Lynn Garner

Driven.

Disconcerted.

Profusely neglected,

Never seemed to fit in.

Mind above the clouds,

Always contemplating the end.

End of envious, and deceitful

Connections...

Starvation of intellection

Maybe I'm too mellow dramatic--

And always reacting...

Nope!

My dream won't be deferred...

Mountains will move before the herd...

Herd of negative energy,

Overwhelming me,

To settle with misery...

Contemplating daily...

Wishing my name was "Kailey"

I would possibly live around more

 "Hailey's"

Yet, dwelling is not the answer,

Tie your tennis shoes and get back to,

Snapping

Snap! Snap!

I'm up!

Never letting up.

Leaving…nah,

Fleeing!

Fleeing from you,

Past me

And tyranny.

Choices are easy.

Paths are hard.

We make shit complicated.

Blood constantly needed

In order to fill the void...

Void of chains,

And to travel, through different

Domains;

To function and breathe

Properly.

So I can still remain,

Driven.

Black Nostalgia   S. Lynn Garner

Black Nostalgia   S. Lynn Garner

Perception

Officially--

Spiritually,

Deliberately-- binding…

Unfiltered, infiltrated, stark; truth,

Haunting instincts; still abiding

Never hiding,

Abstract proof.

Yet, answers clearly—

As the waters of Peru.

Delicately… fleeting,

Instantly speaking,

Yet, tragically seeking…

Too busy thinking.

Judgments form,

Which starts the storm

So uncouth.

Black Nostalgia   S. Lynn Garner

Black Nostalgia   S. Lynn Garner

Stagnant

Haven't forgotten,

Still rotten...

You always had a chance,

Mad from a stance.

Keep your heart clear

You're still entangled in fear

It's okay to smear…

But character is calling

And you are on the edge,

Possibly falling,

Never pursuing

Just renewing...

Old traits, and old ways

Too bad

You have to stay!

Stay in time…

We aren't aligned.

Paths diverged

Since,

I had the courage

To leave you,

Behind.

Black Nostalgia   S. Lynn Garner

Black Nostalgia   S. Lynn Garner

Potion

Taste my secrets

Keep me beaming

Sweetest demon

Slow – deep dreaming

Iridescent glow

Friend or pretty foe

Sings me praises

Keeps me patiently waiting

Black Nostalgia   S. Lynn Garner

Temptress sin

Jaded nights on end.

Dripping heart beats

Seem to win; kindred grins

Wakes me screaming

Leaves me timid

Yet - ever a fiend

NY trips; I'm scheming

Still believing.

S. Lynn Garner

S. Lynn Garner

Intentional

Random views dismissed

Pin pointed hearts exist

In my mind of bliss

Never will I blunder this

Substance is the goal

As beauty unfolds

Never will I go

Back to temporary moments of glow

Deep rooted connections

Never will I once again neglect

Mind of rituals

And true intellect

A moment in time

Can fuck up a light so bright

Tender moments of affection

Can set up of a life of missed direction

Following who?

Serendipitous foes, and fools

Never will I neglect

My standards and rules

Empty levels of hope

Forms a hollow, forgotten soul

Moments of regretful no's

Never will I sell my heart for show

Speaking out for fun

Staining reputation to some

Having the last word; so done

Never will I waste time for one.

Mind in the clouds

Time to bring back down

Down to earth

And create solid worth

Conscious or not

Time still ticks on the clock

You only have one shot

Until you are permanently forgot

Choices are free

Solid seeds in your toolbox of dreams

Use intuitions properly

And live your destiny

Peaceful Reflections

Black Nostalgia   S. Lynn Garner

Black Nostalgia   S. Lynn Garner

"The greatest glory in living lies in never failing, but in rising every time we fail."

-Nelson Mandela

"You may not control all the events that happen to you, but you can decide not to be reduced by them"

-Maya Angelou

Black Nostalgia

S. Lynn Garner

"If you don't understand yourself, you don't understand anybody else.

-Nicki Giovanni

"The only way you can grow is to let yourself make mistakes and create contradictions. As we learn new things, some of our old attitudes will change."

-Nikki Giovanni

"I have learned that success is to be measured not so much by the position that one has reached in life as by the obstacles which he has overcome while trying to succeed."

-Booker T. Washington

"Challenges make you discover things about yourself, that you never really knew."

-Cicely Tyson

"If you're walking down the right path and you're willing to keep walking, eventually you'll make progress"

-Barack Obama

"Change will not come if we wait for some other person or some other time. We are the ones we've been waiting for. We are the change that we seek."

-Barack Obama

"I have learned that success is to be measured not so much by the position that one has reached in life as by the obstacles which he has overcome while trying to succeed."

-Booker T. Washington

"Go to work! Go to work in the morn of a new creation... until you have... reached the height of self-progress, and from that pinnacle bestow upon the world a civilization of your own."

-Marcus Garvey

*"It's not the load that breaks you
down, it's the way you carry it."*

-Lena Horne

"You wanna fly, you got to give up the shit that weighs you down."

-Toni Morrison

Black Nostalgia

S. Lynn Garner

"If I didn't define myself for myself, I would be crunched into other people's fantasies for me and eaten alive."

-Audre Lorde

"Not everything that is faced can be changed; but nothing can be changed until it is faced."

-James Baldwin

"It is the mind that makes the body."

-**Sojourner Truth**

"The most common way people give up their power is by thinking they don't have any."

-Alice Walker

Black Nostalgia   S. Lynn Garner

*"I don't think God created us, to sit
with our hands tied, and our mouths
closed. Search your soul, and you will
find the truth. Progress and self-
worth, will be conquered."*

-S. Lynn Garner

S. Lynn Garner

Acknowledgment

I thank God for allowing me to live in my purpose. I truly hope my words will empower others to live their best lives; unapologetically. I'm beyond thankful for my supportive family. My heart will be bonded to my loves forever.

I also would like to thank everyone I personally connected with, through both business, and personal travels. It was an absolute pleasure to collaborate, and network with some of the most influential individuals across the globe. I'm definitely more inspired to take risks, and live out my dreams, through purposeful intent.

I'm appreciative for the complexities of life, and its profound lessons.

-S. Lynn Garner

About the Author

About the Author

S. Lynn Garner, is an African-American
Author, with Southern Louisiana roots;
residing in Houston, Texas. She holds a
B.A. in English, with an emphasis in
rhetoric, from Texas A&M University, and a
M.A. in Liberal Arts Philosophy/Sociology,
from Texas Christian University. S. Lynn
Garner currently works as an International
Baccalaureate Programme Coordinator,
content creator, and freelance writer. S.
Lynn Garner, specializes in ELA, and ESL
teacher instructional coaching, and is a
member of the Pearson SIOP Advisory
Panel. She enjoys traveling, and spending
time with her family. Please visit
lynngarner.com for more information.

Stories Untold

Series

The "Stories Untold" series travels through an intimate, endearing; nostalgic journey, once forgotten. Themes unraveled: progress, discernment, ambition, gratitude, and much more.

Black Nostalgia

Black Nostalgia II (A Spiritual Remedy)

Books by This Author

-**Black Nostalgia**

-**Black Nostalgia II (A Spiritual Remedy)**

-**Brooke Goes to Kindergarten**

 (A Brookie Cookie Series)

Notes:

Notes:

Notes:

Notes:

Notes:

Made in the USA
Columbia, SC
28 July 2020

14921755R00114